Cute
FLOWERS

GRAYSCALE COLORING BOOKS

VOLUME 2.

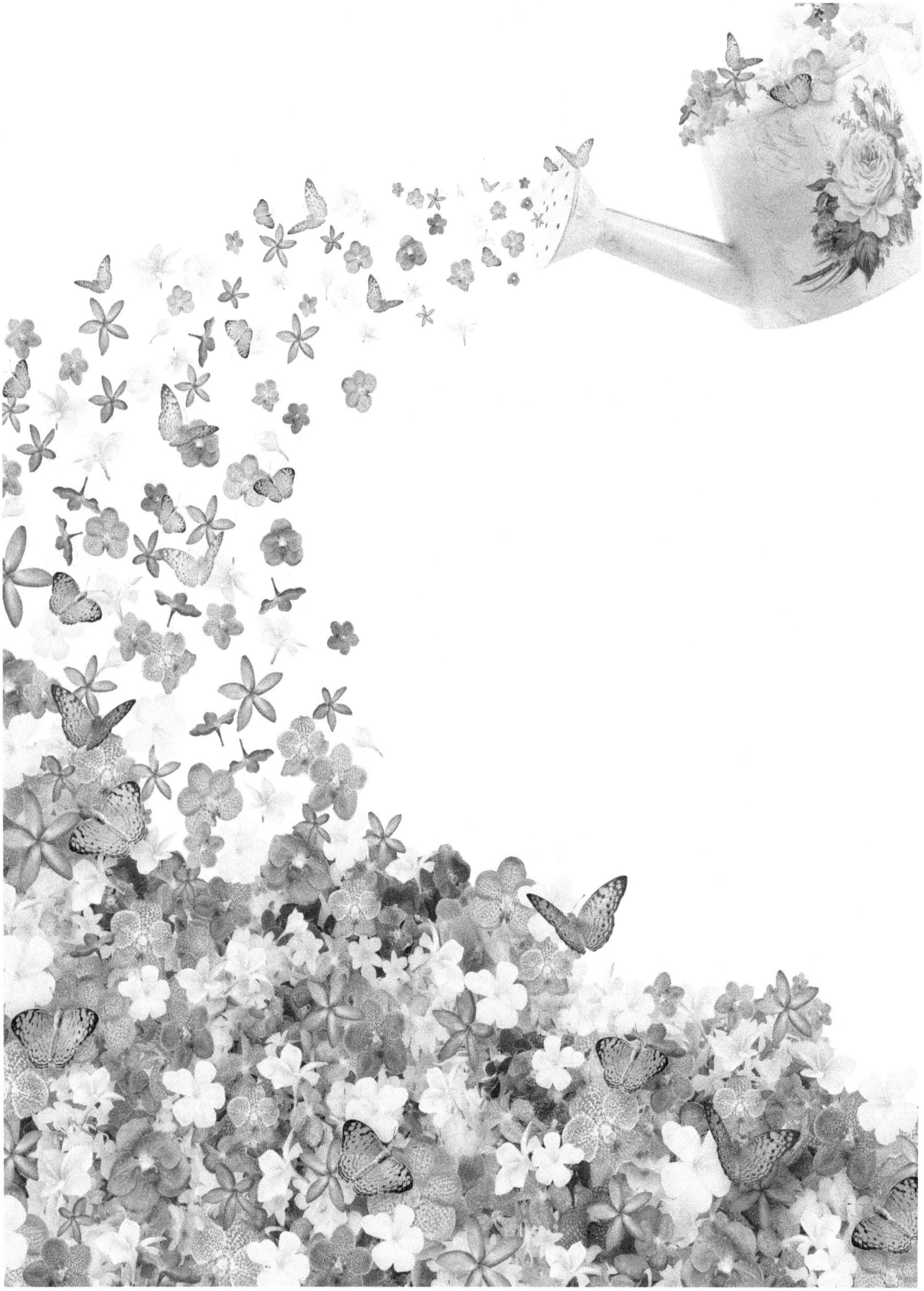

COLOR TEST PAGE

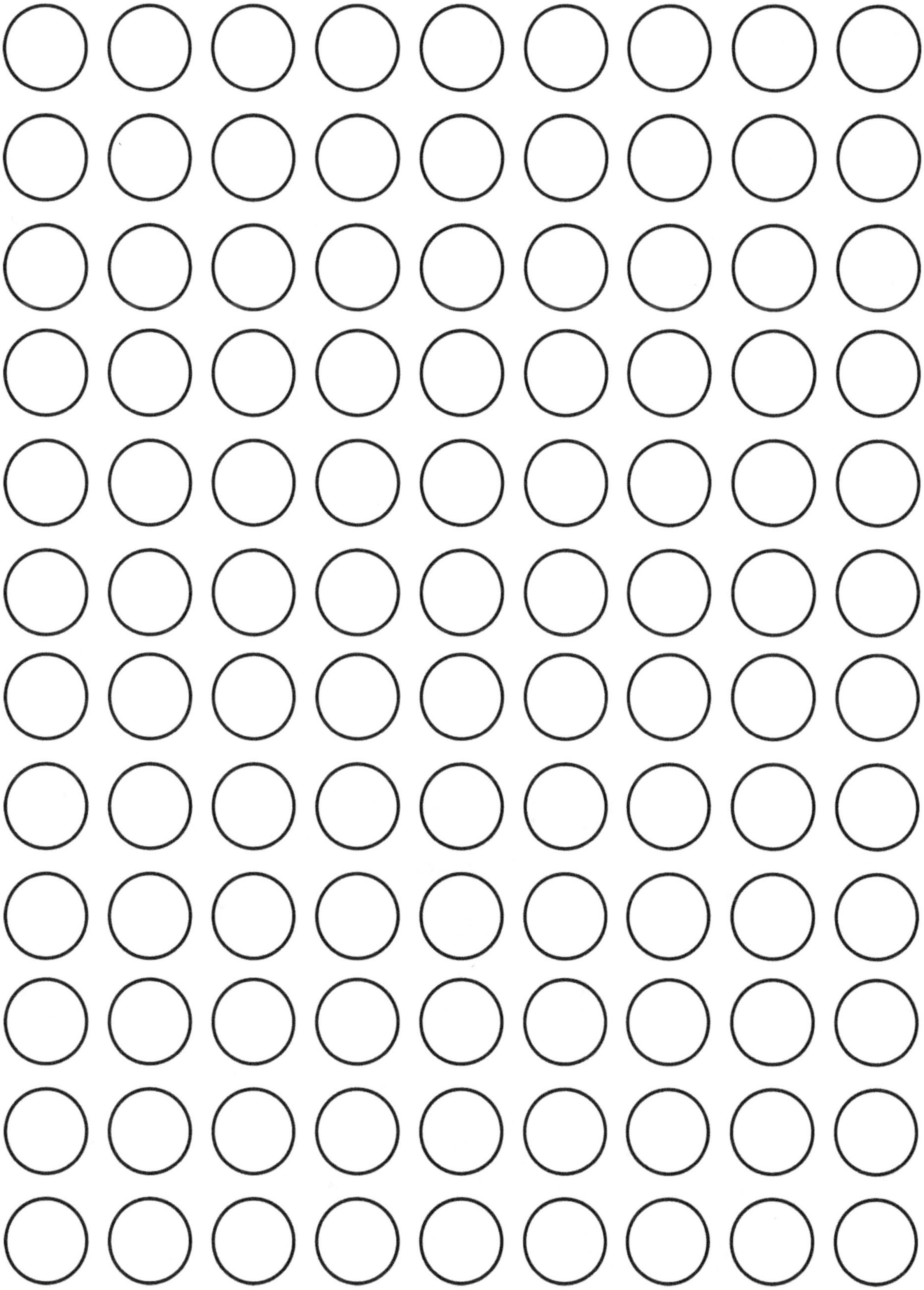

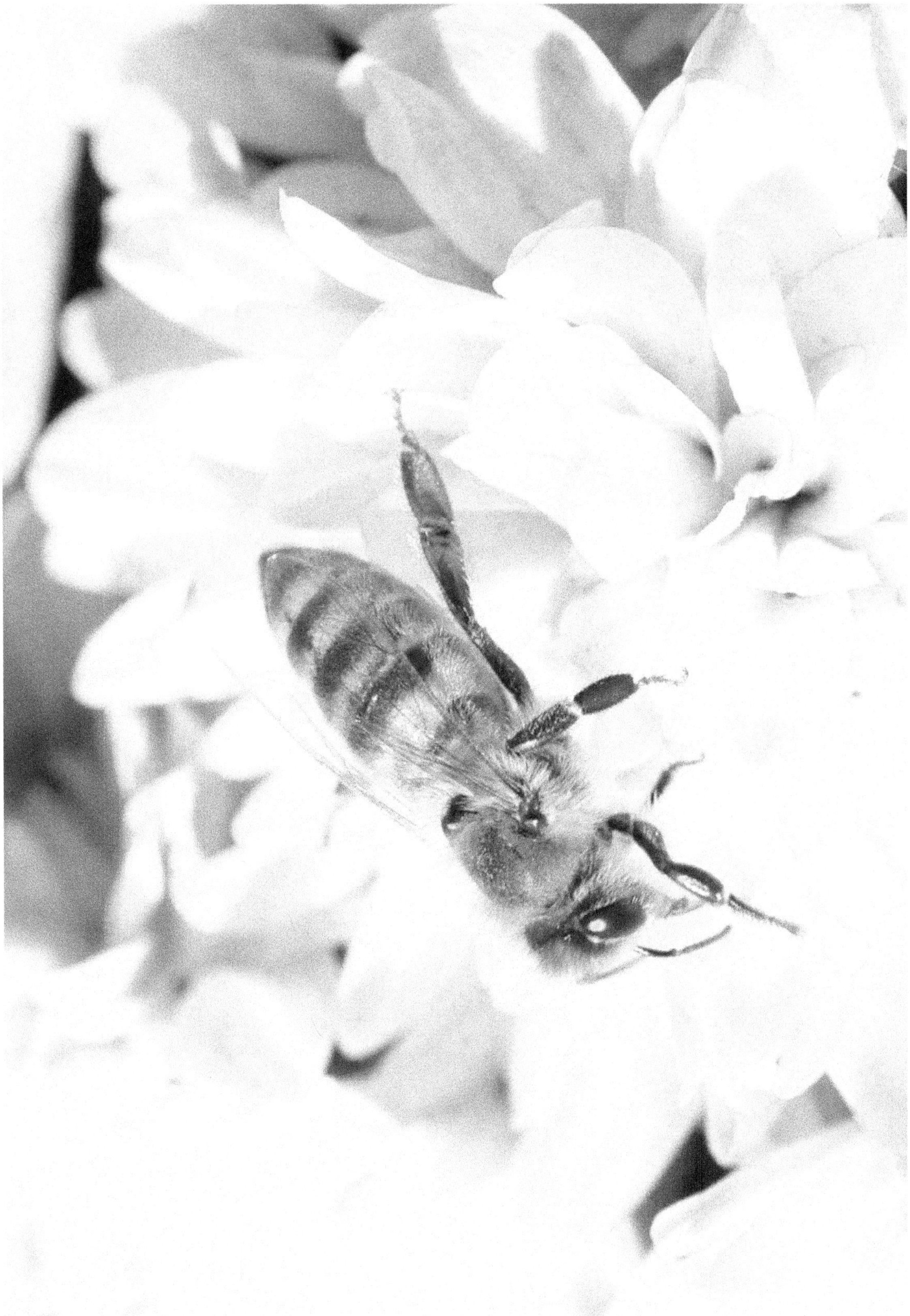

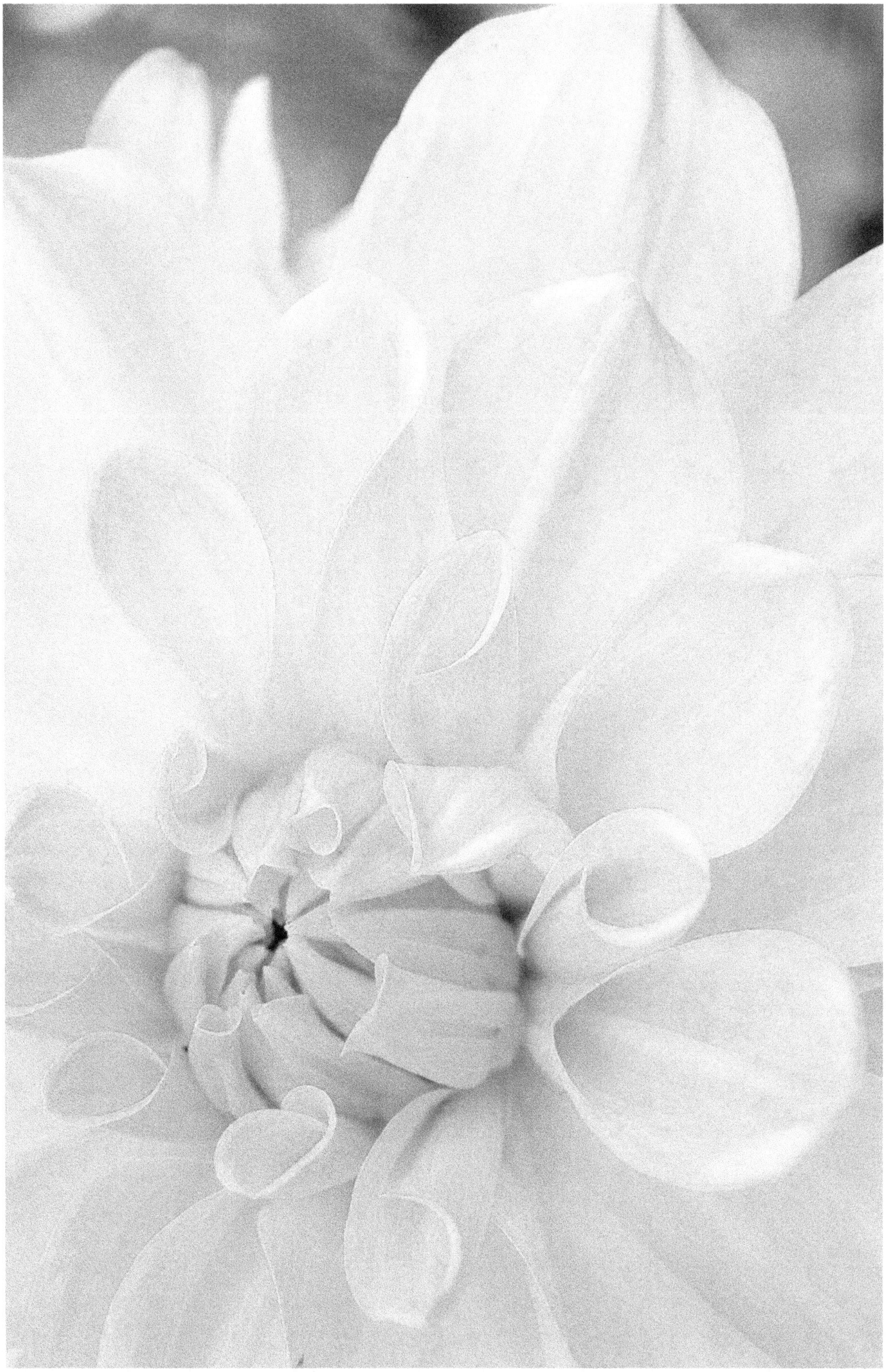

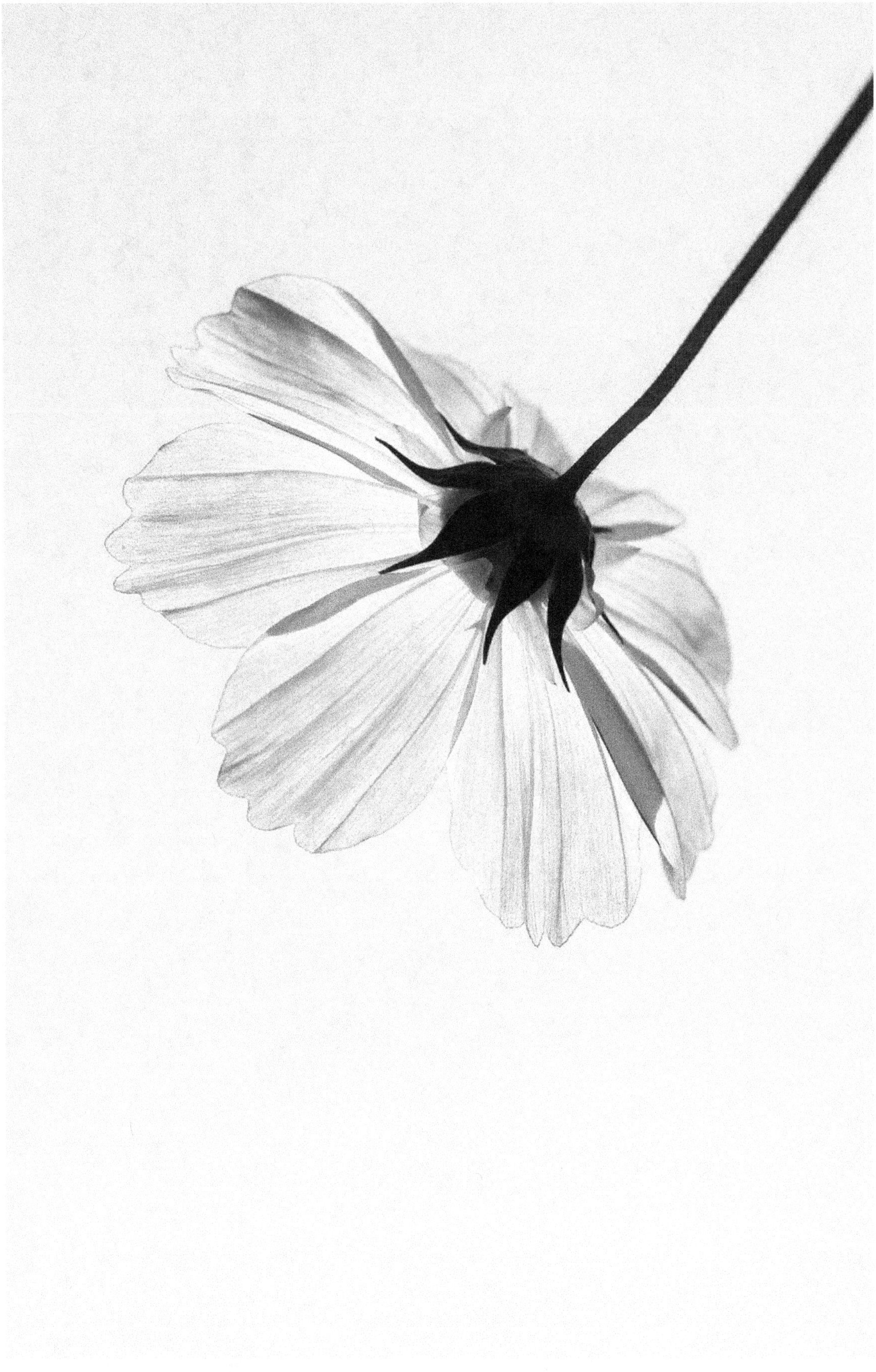

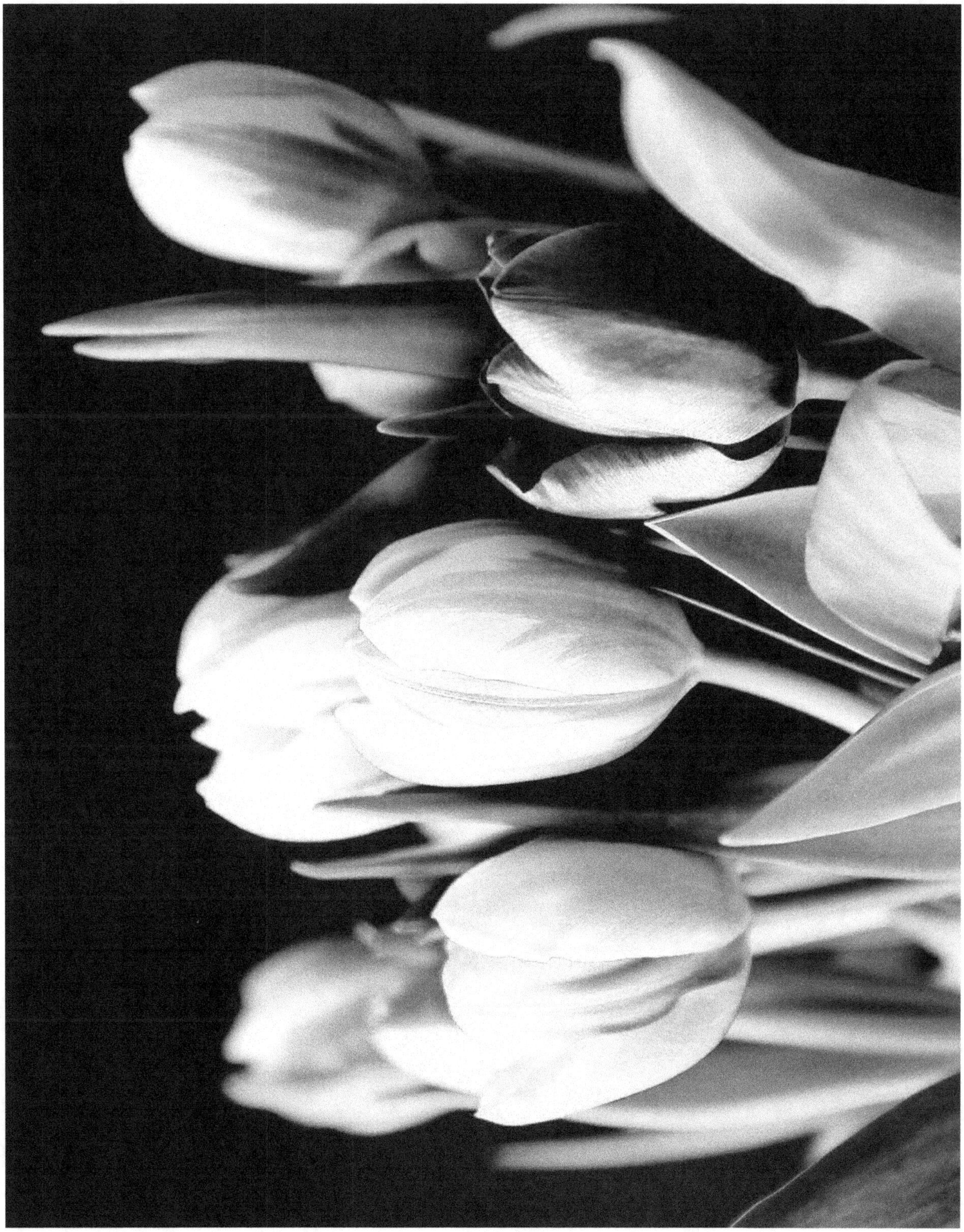

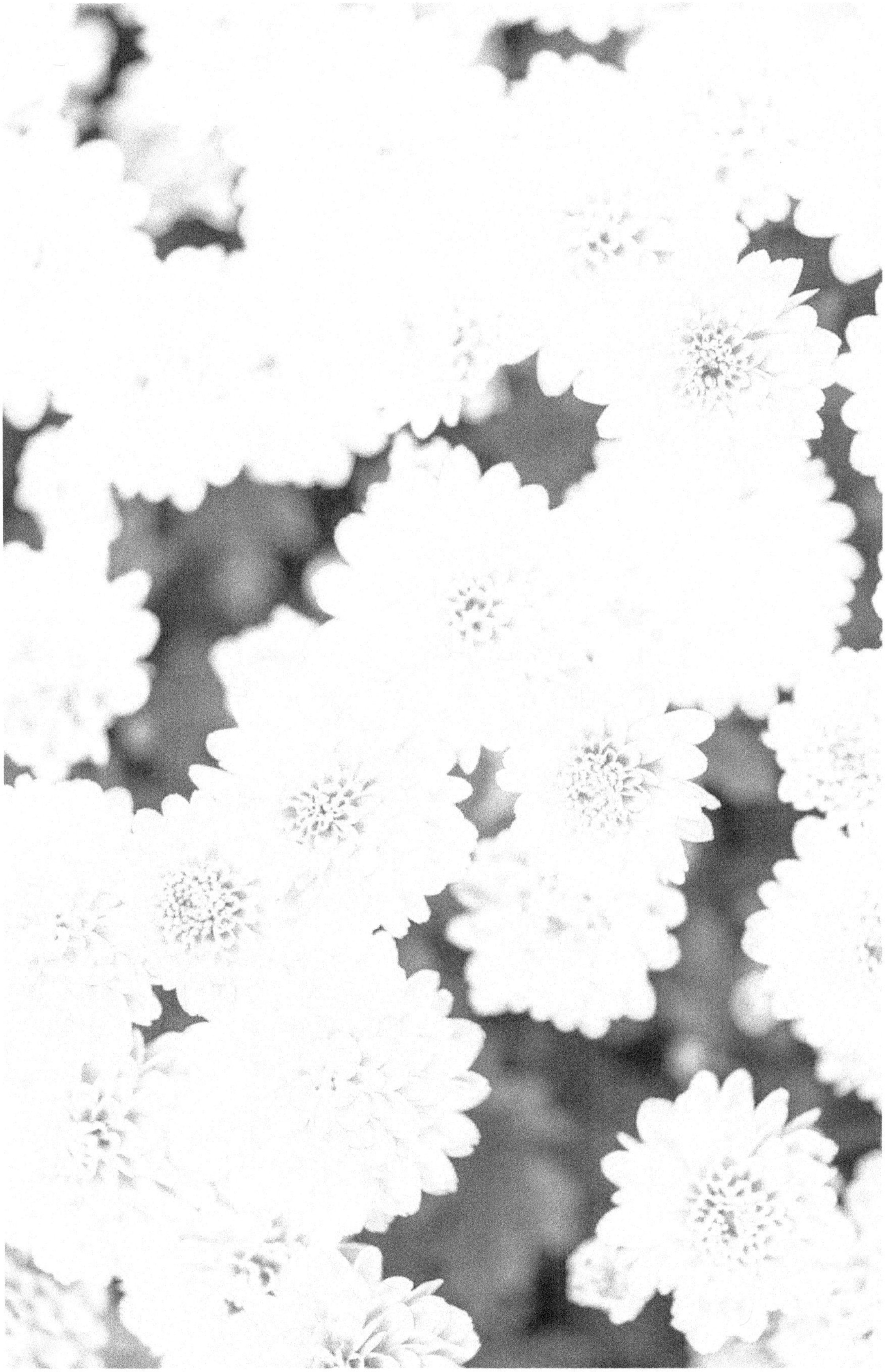

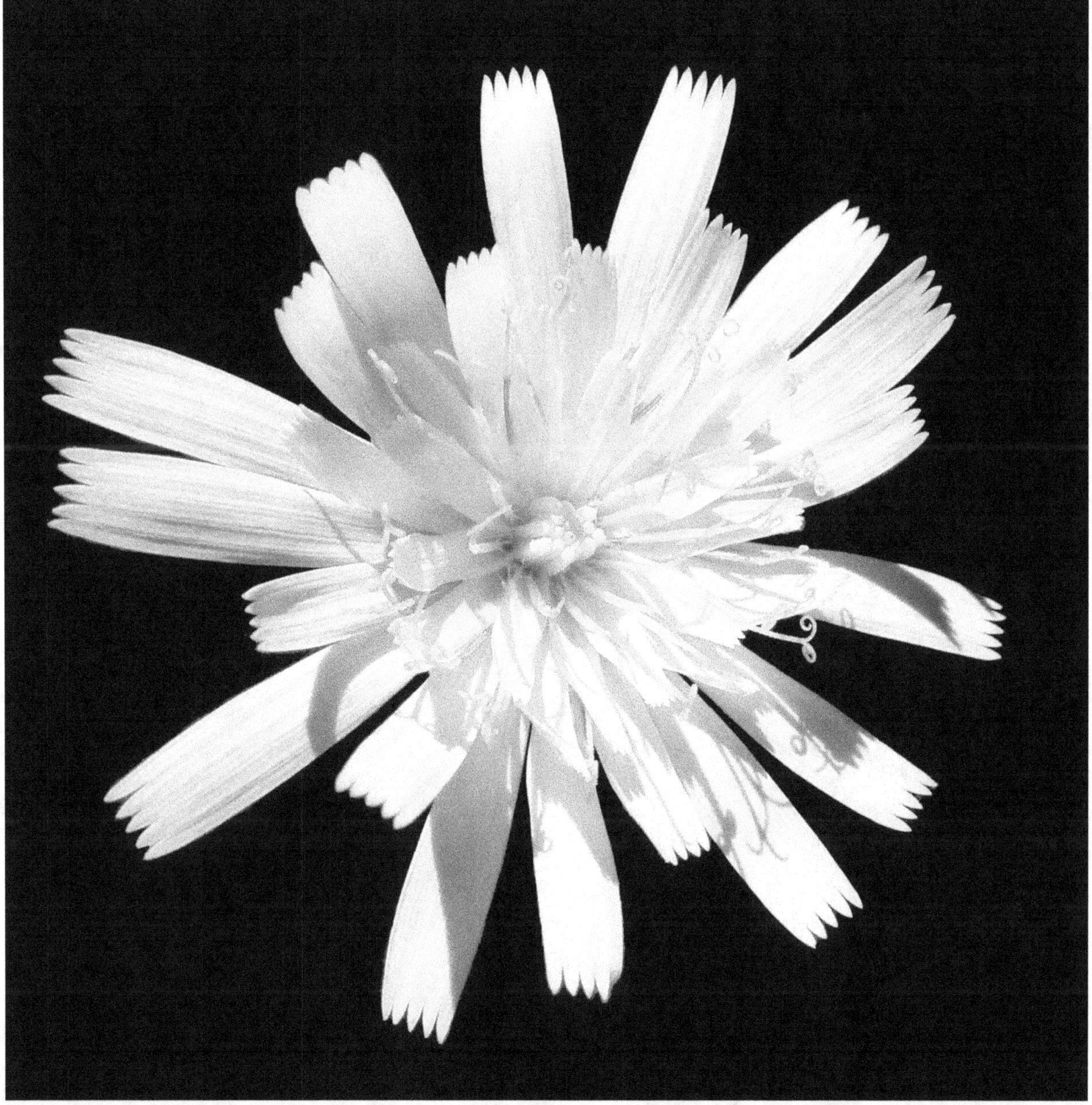

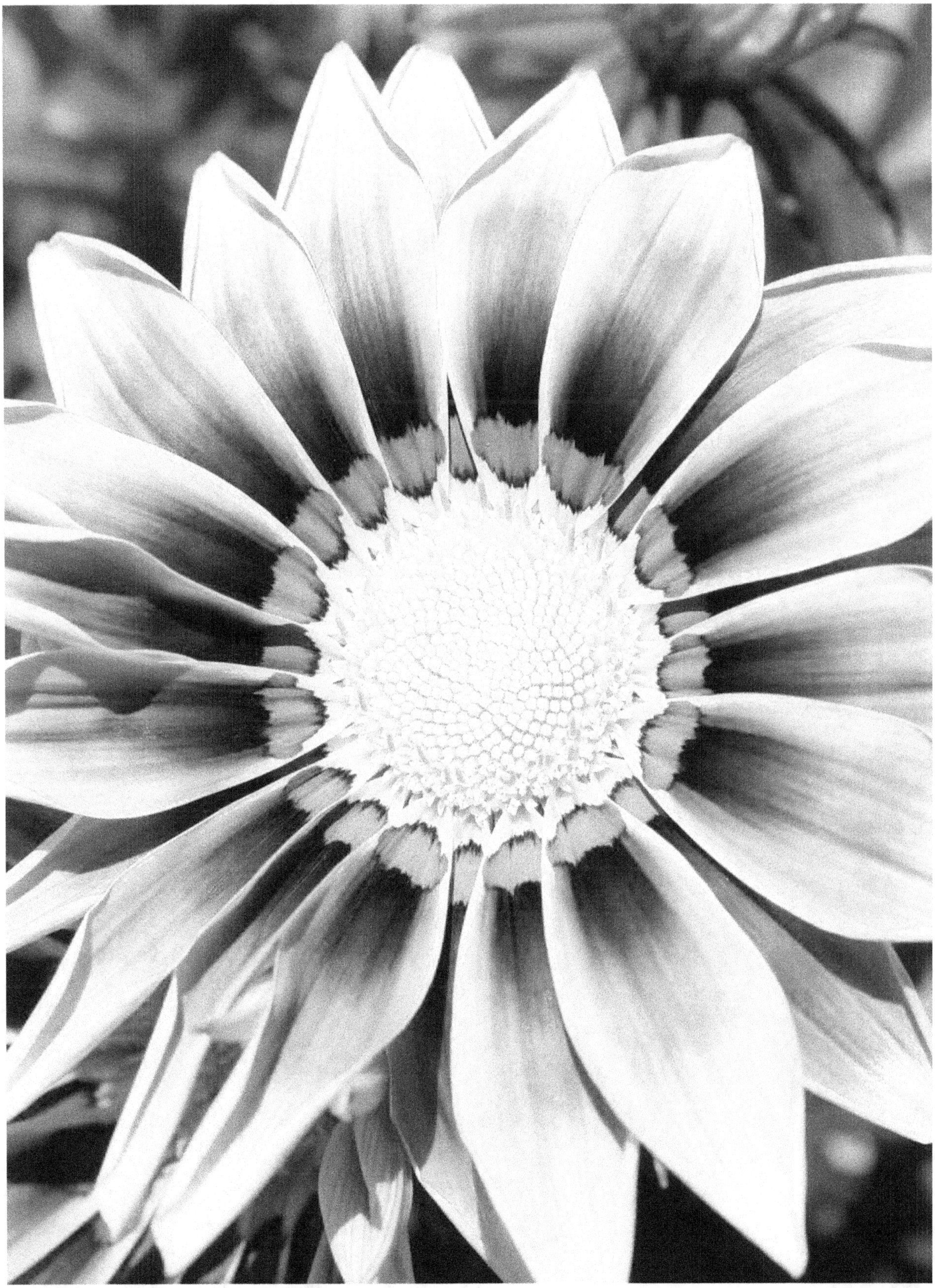

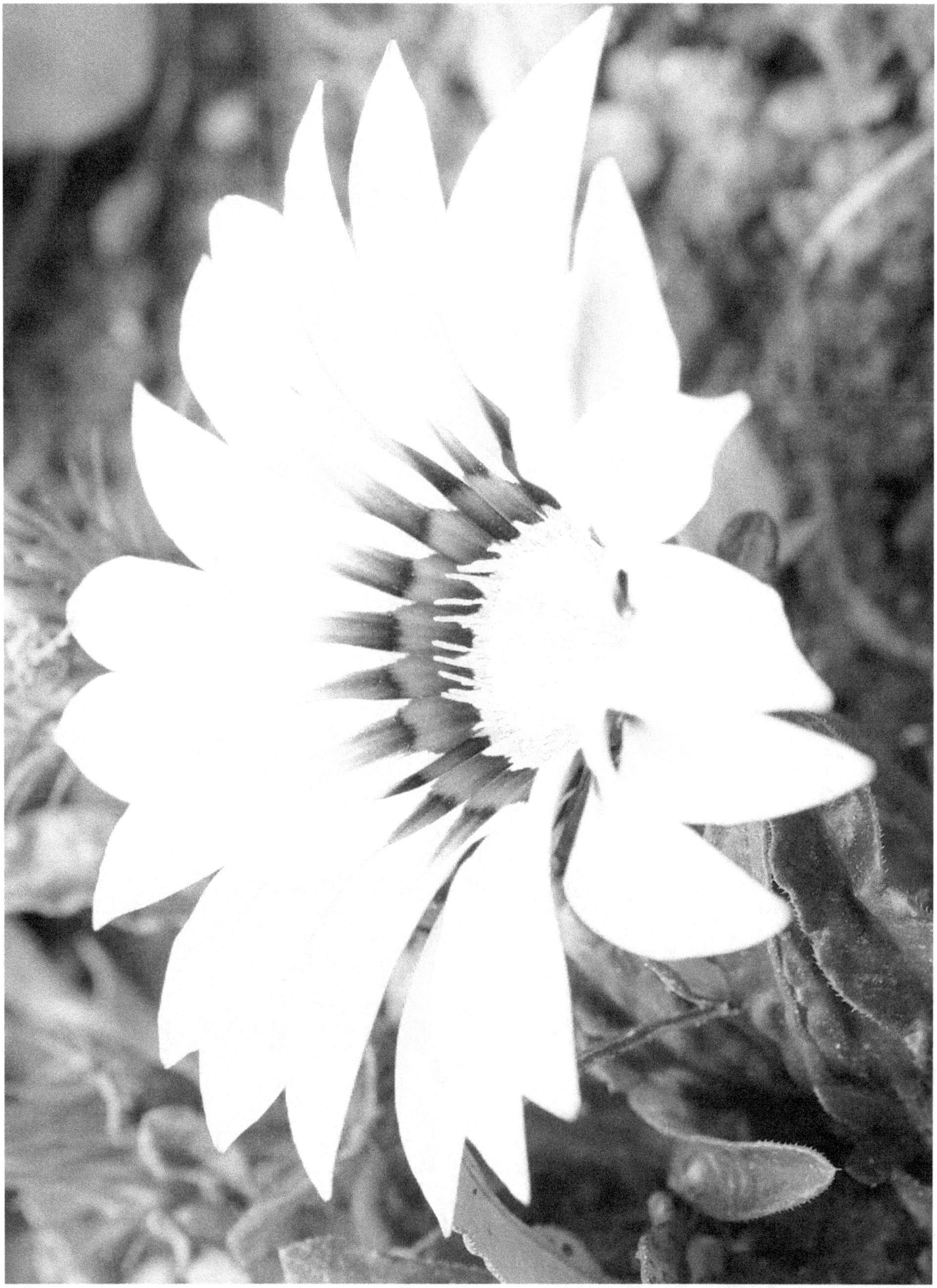

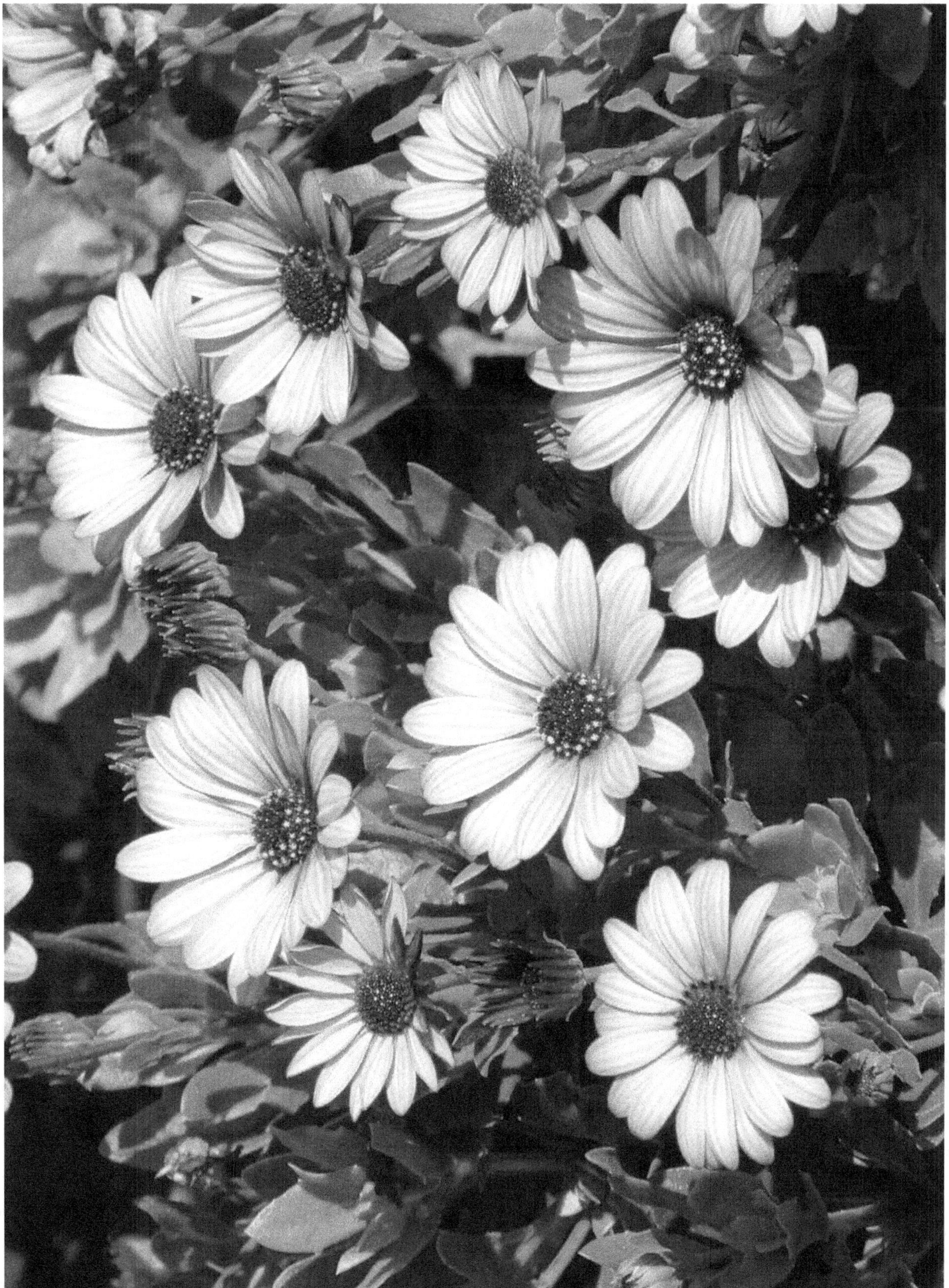

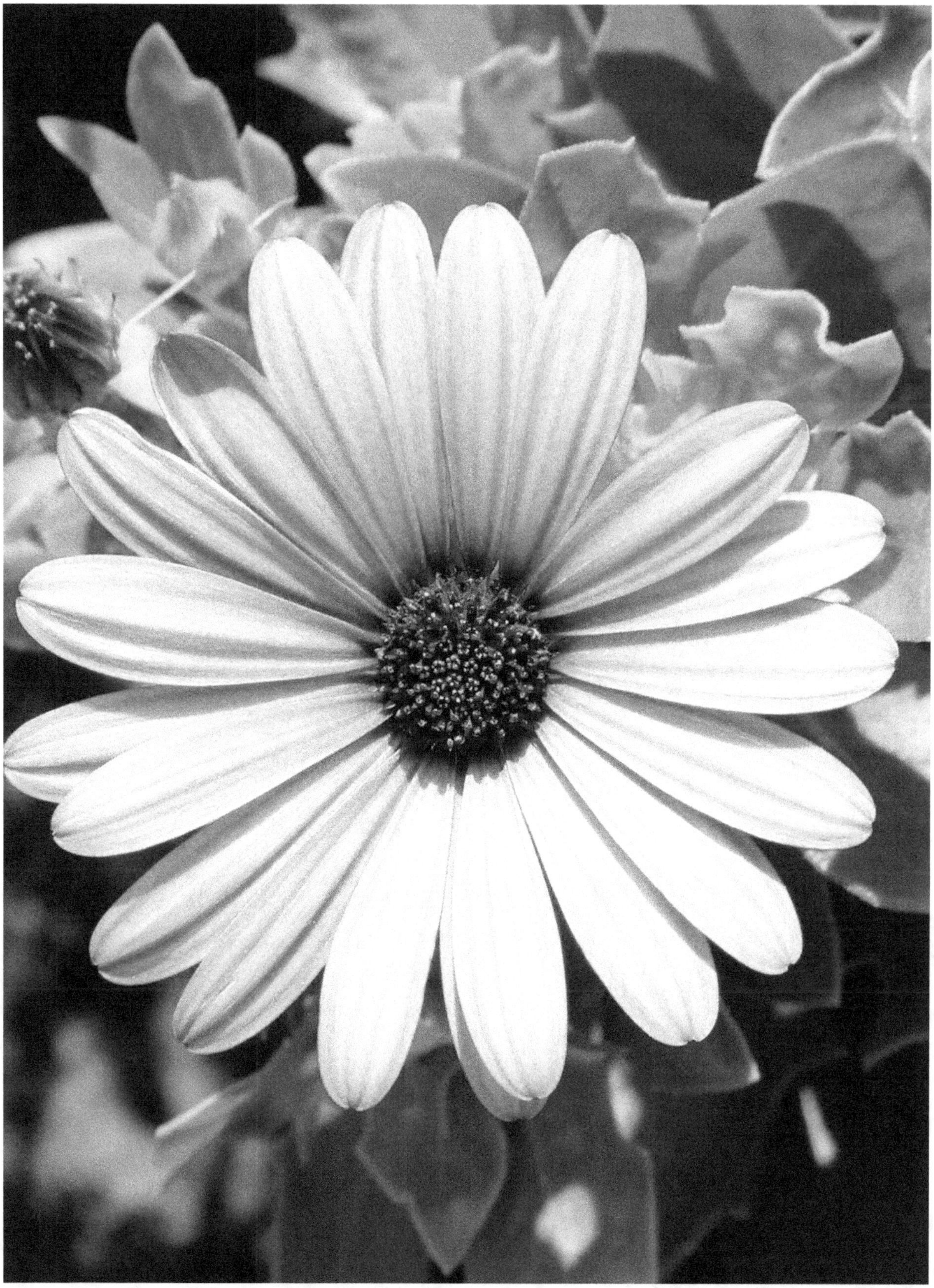

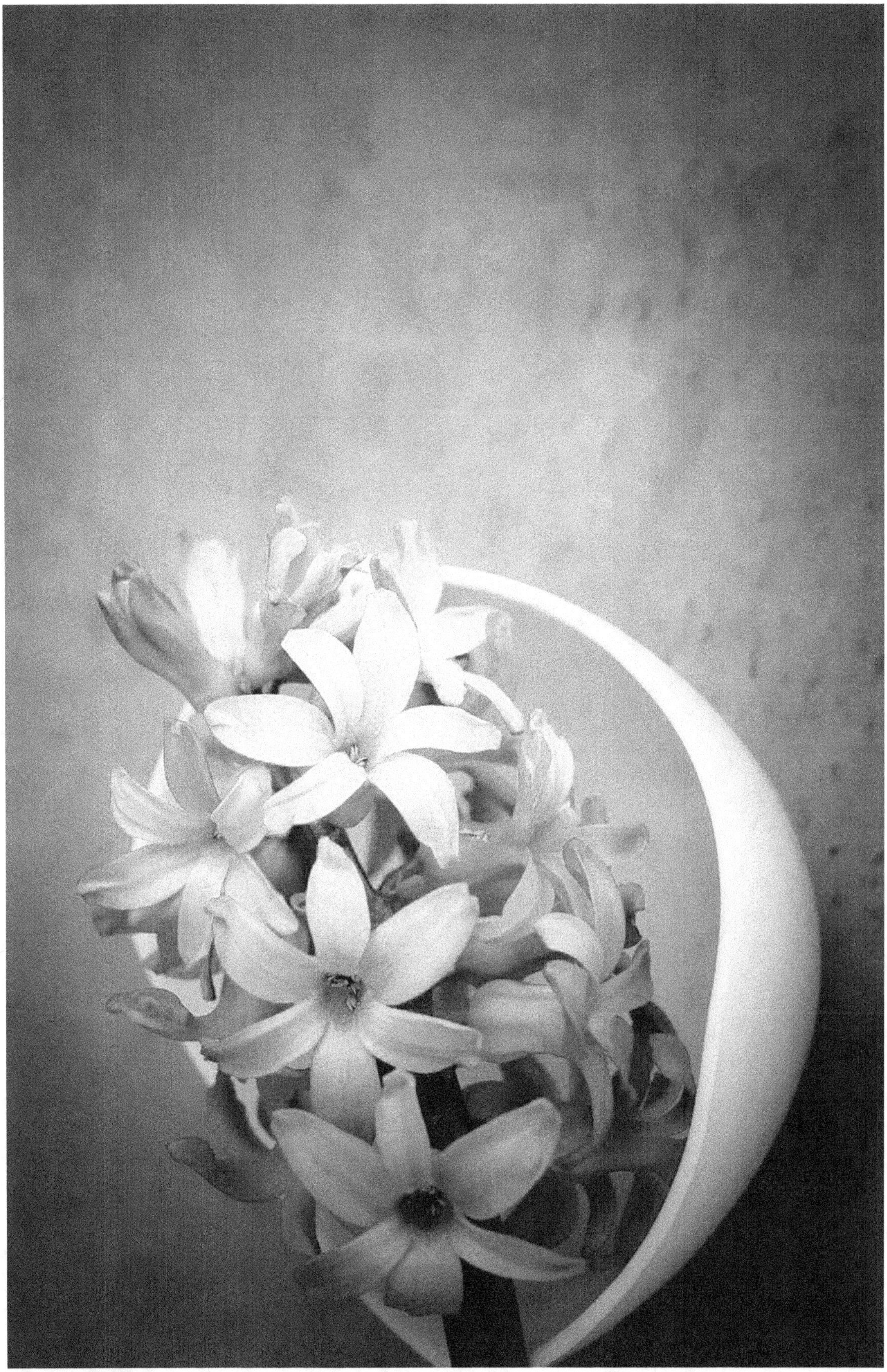

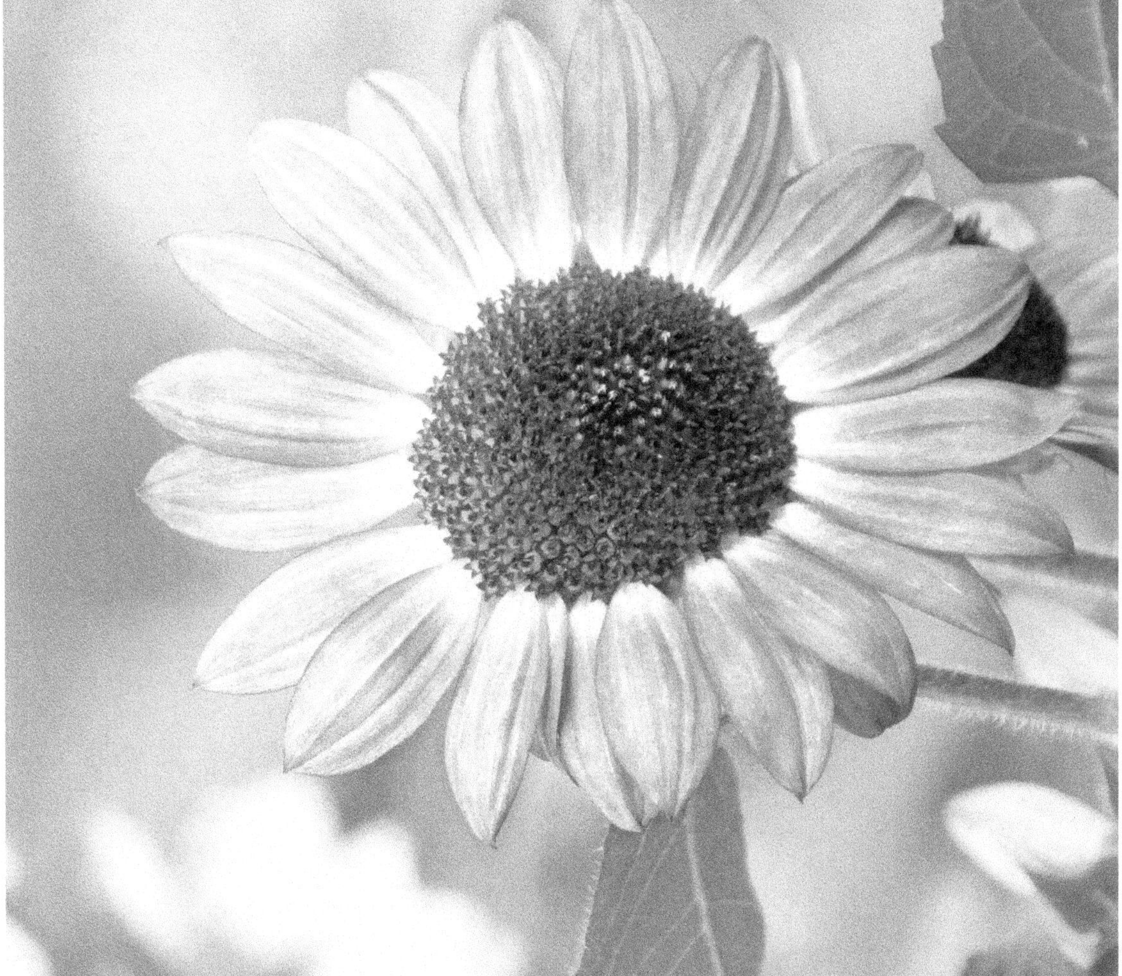

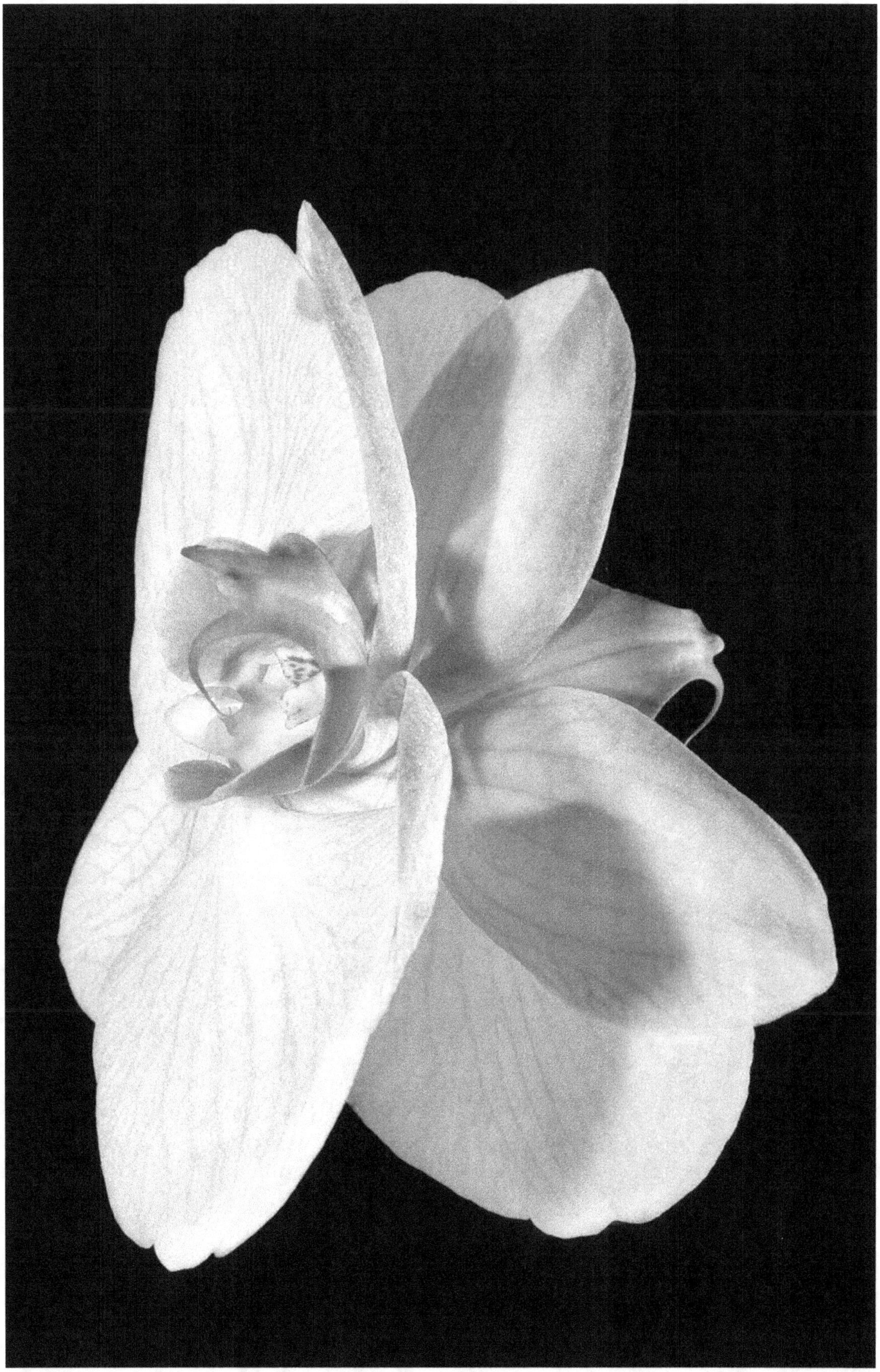

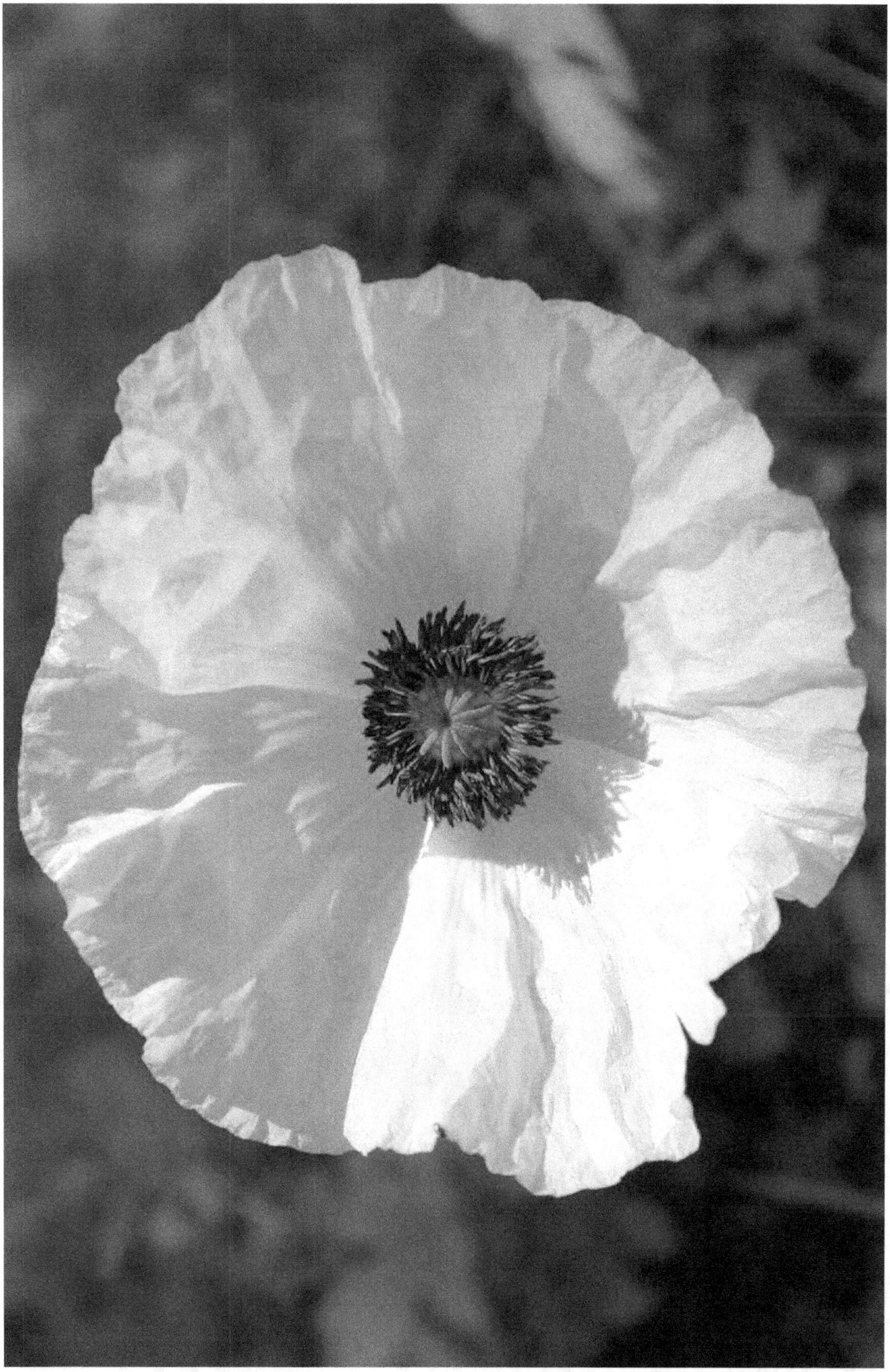

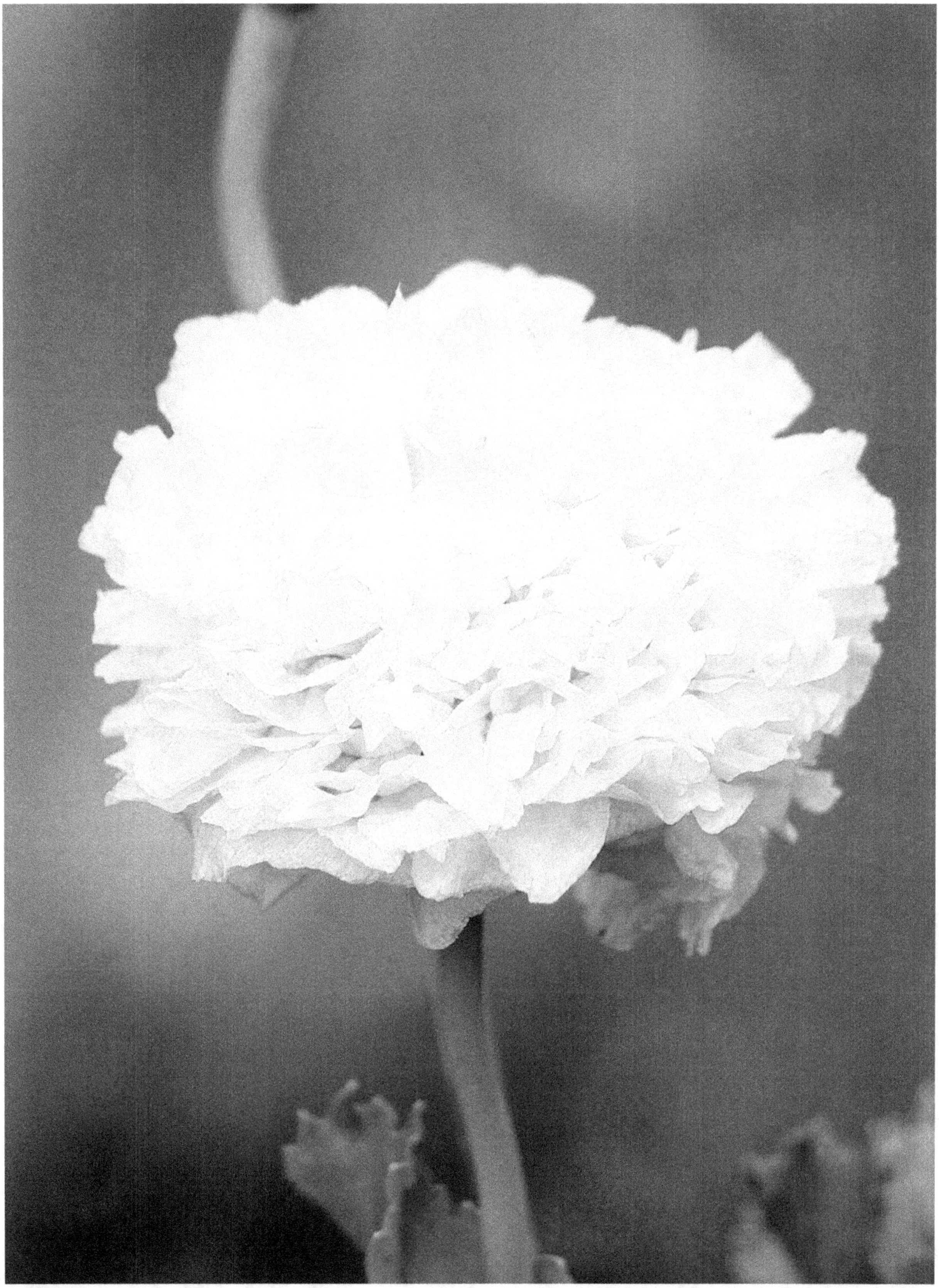

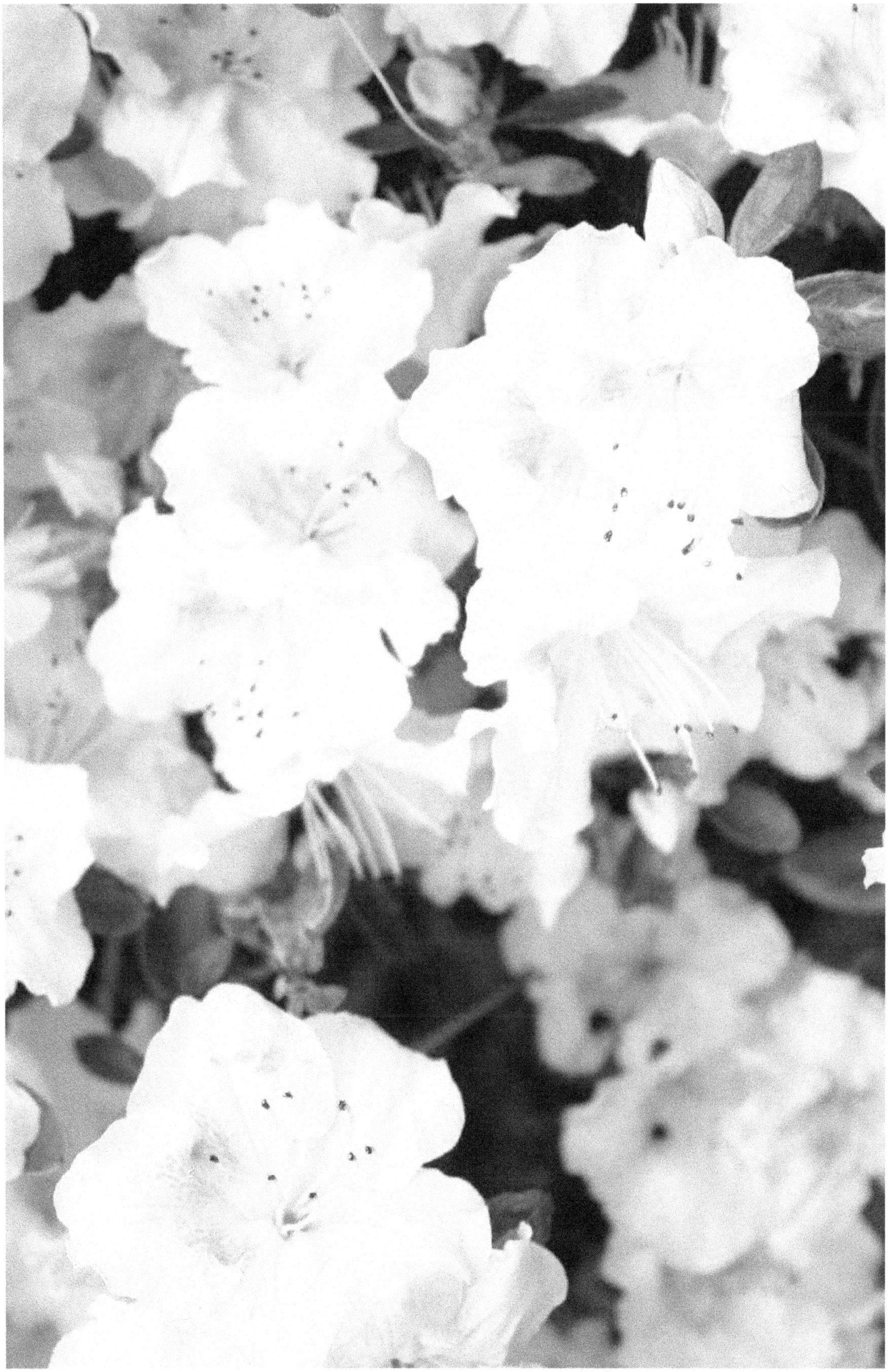

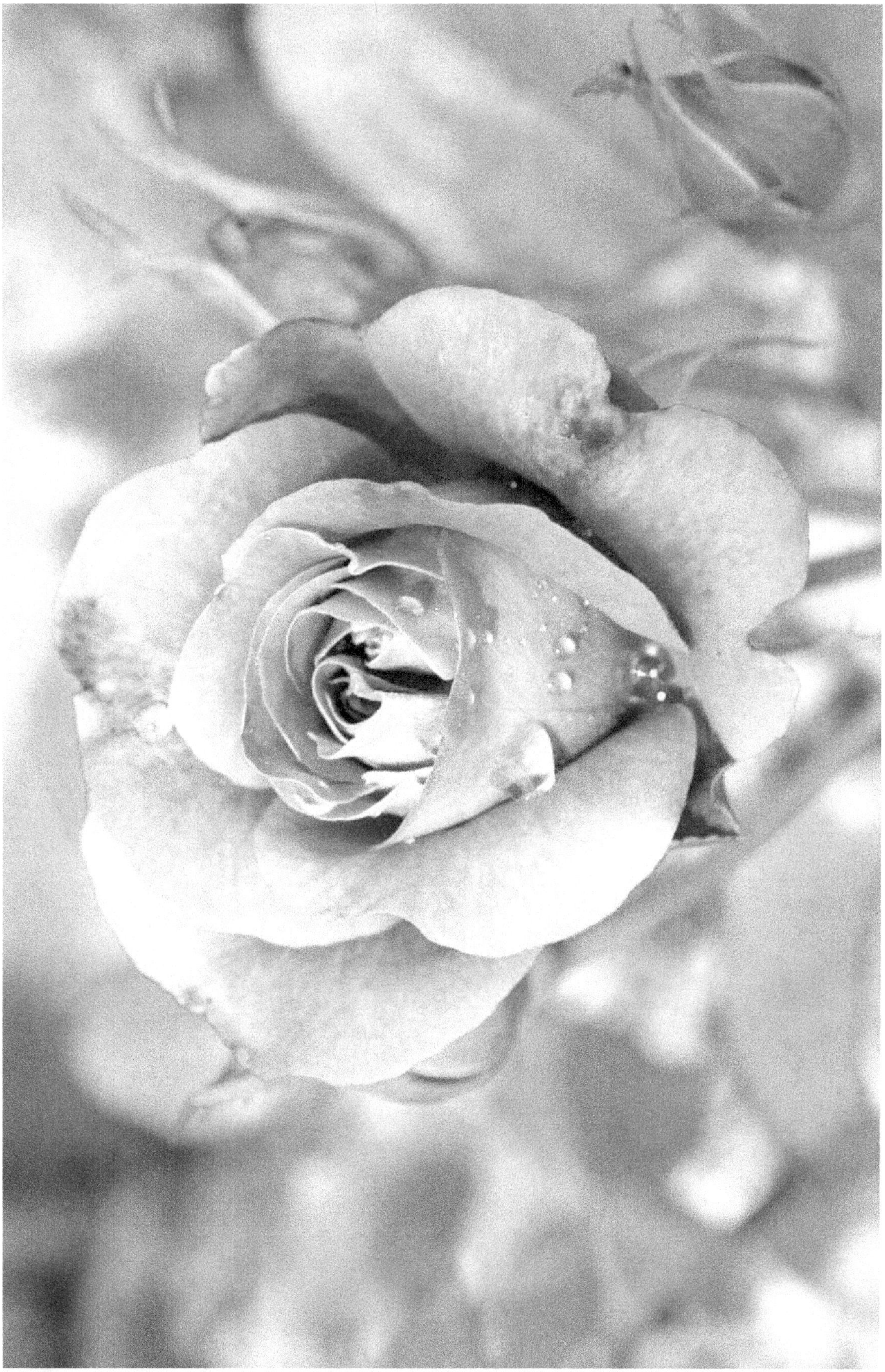

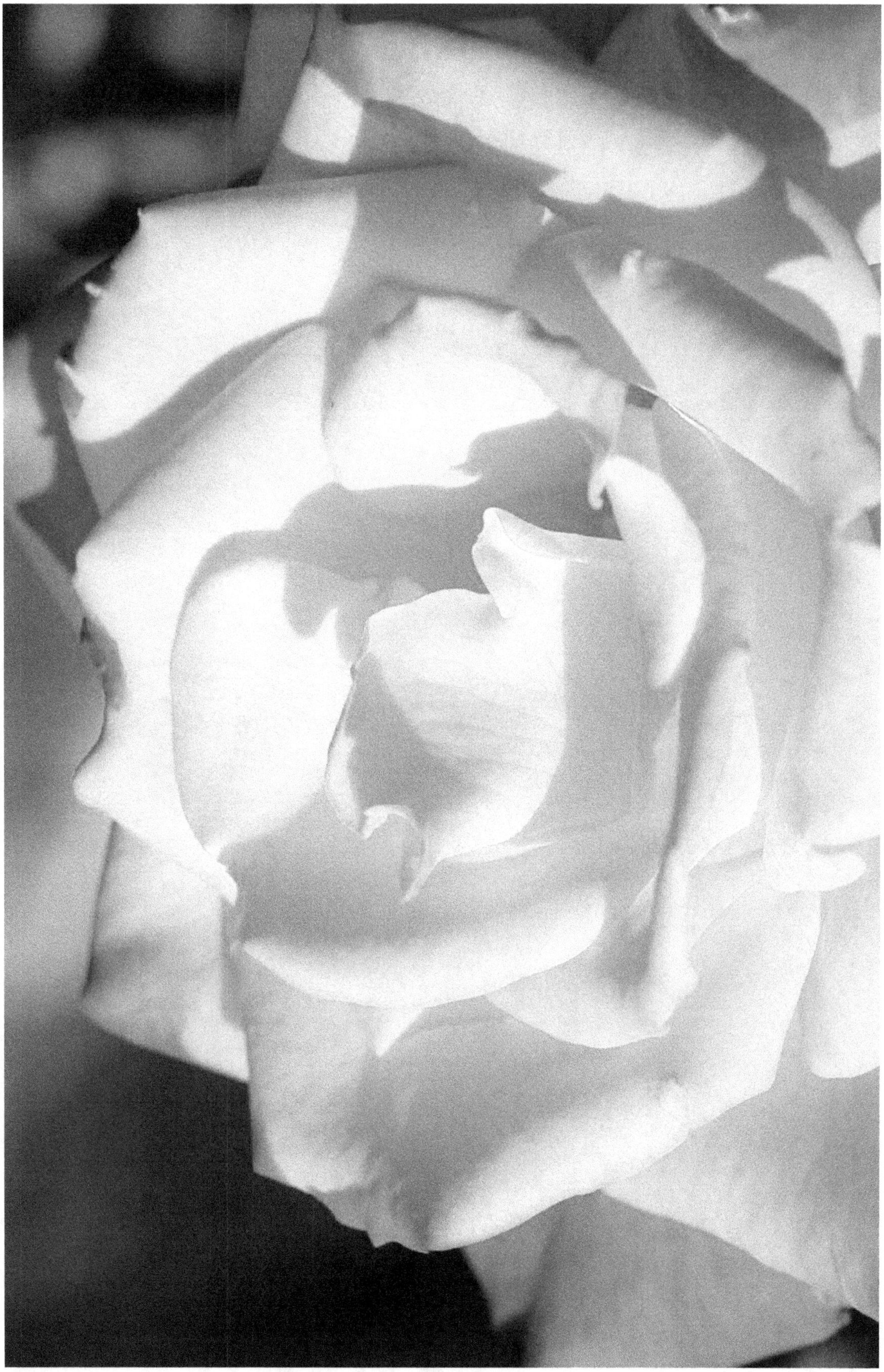

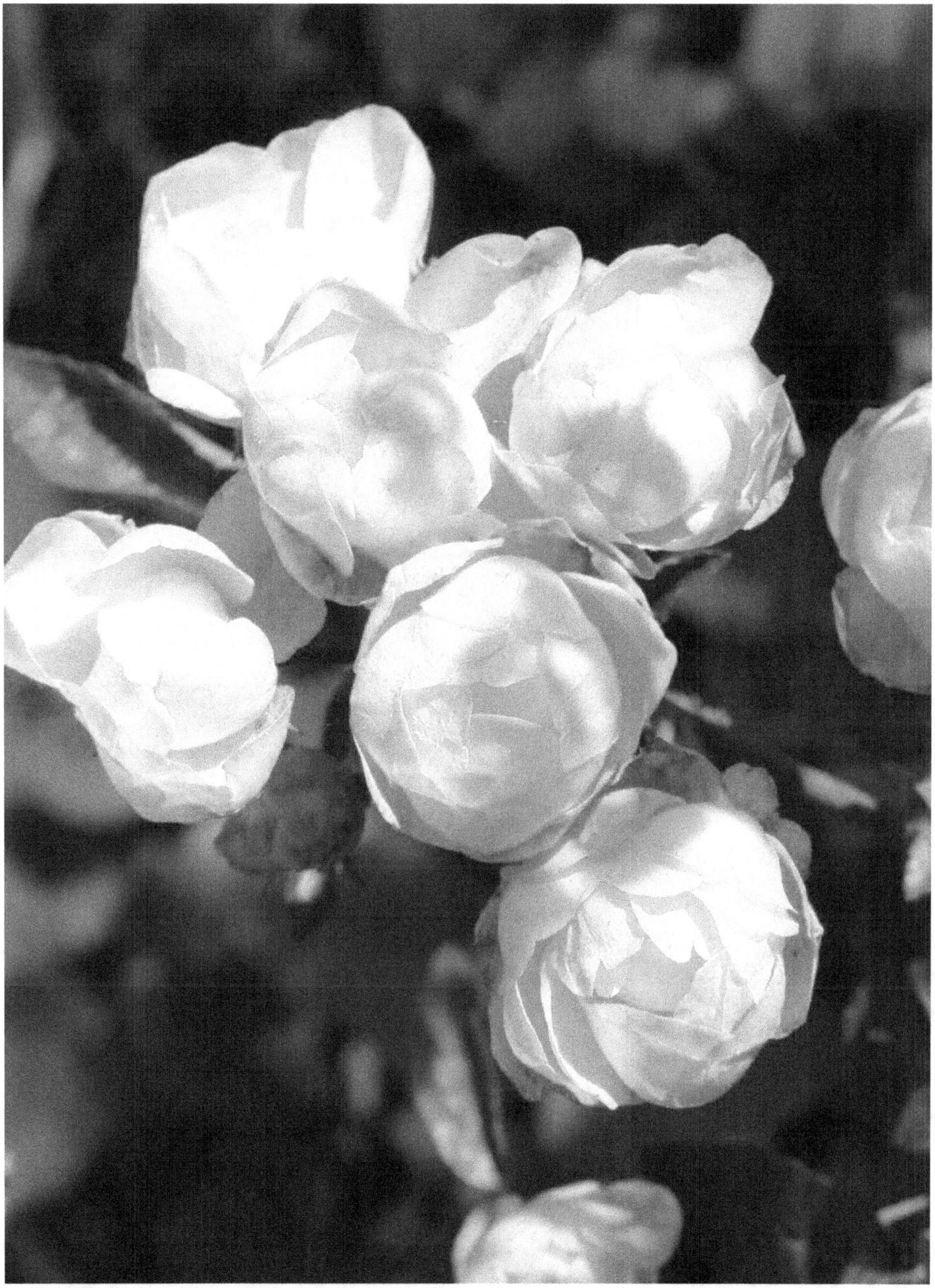

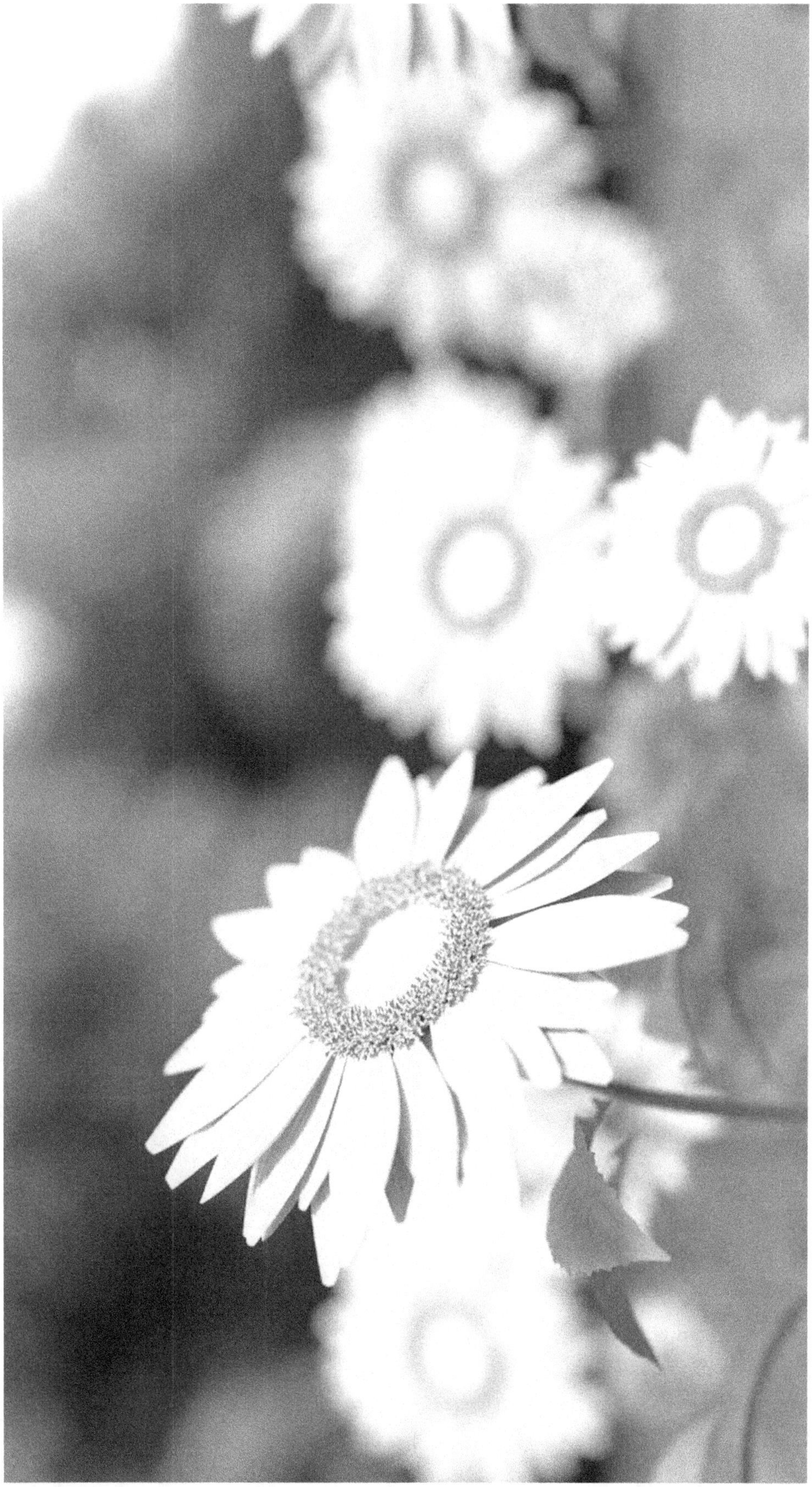

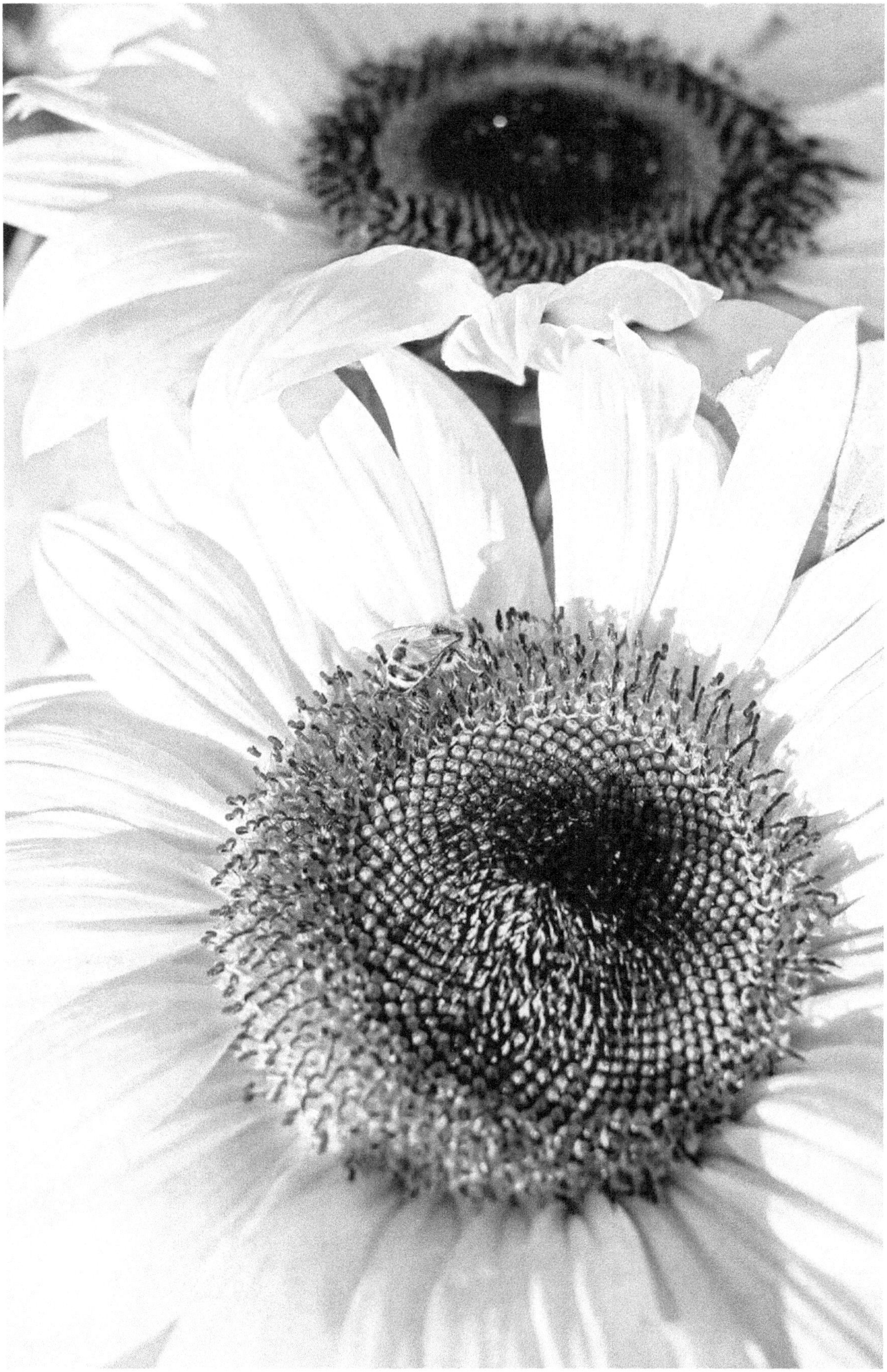

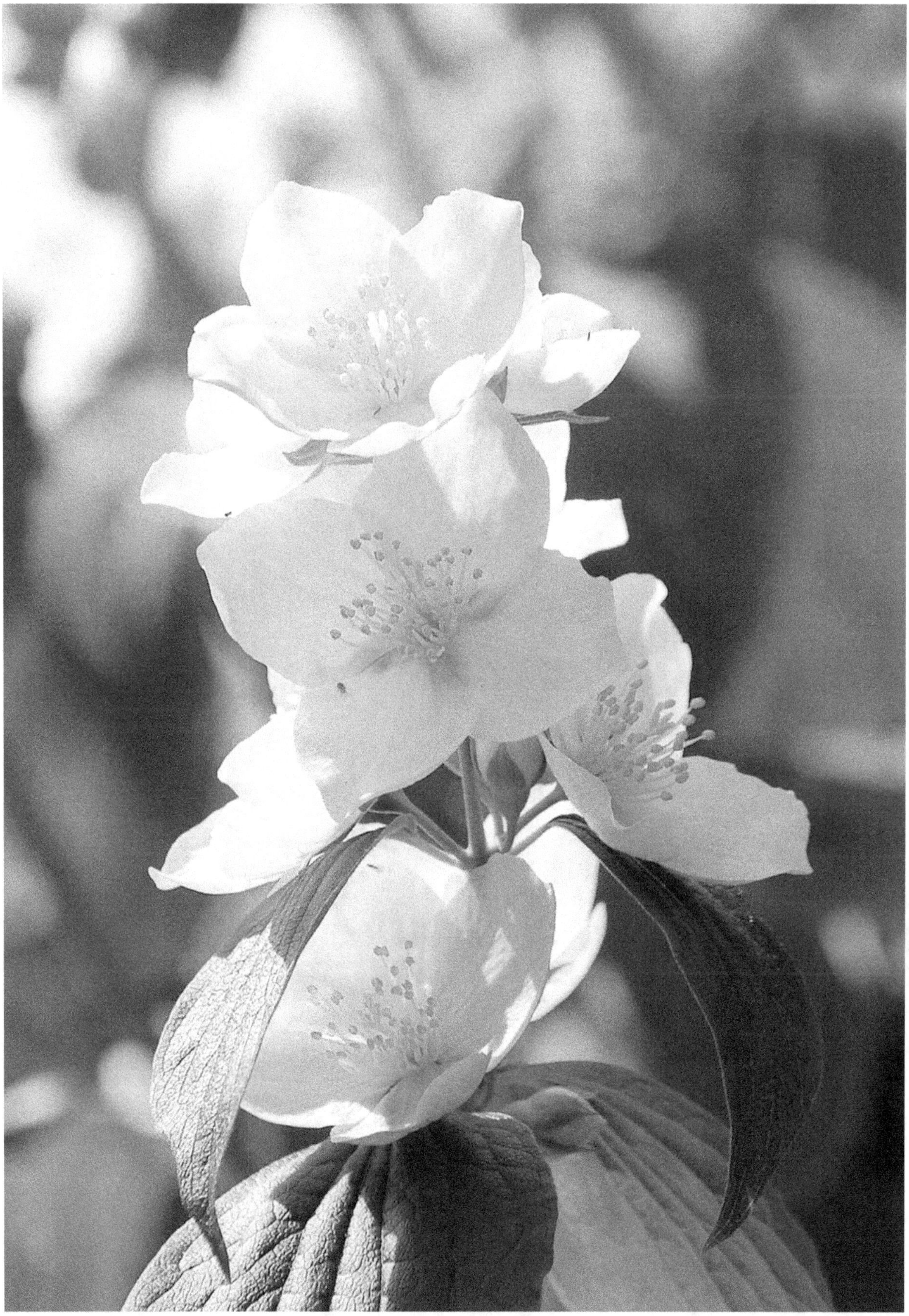

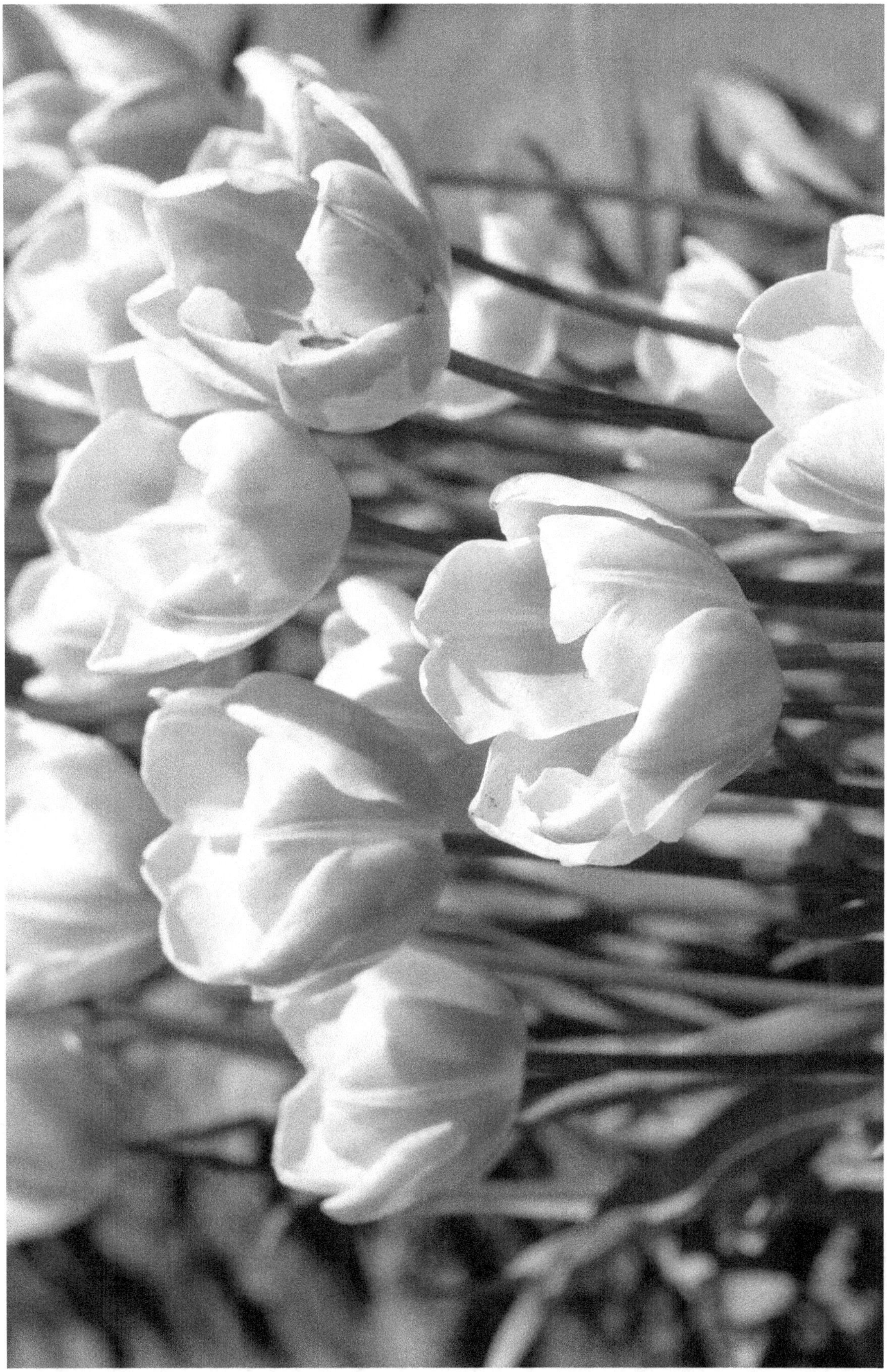

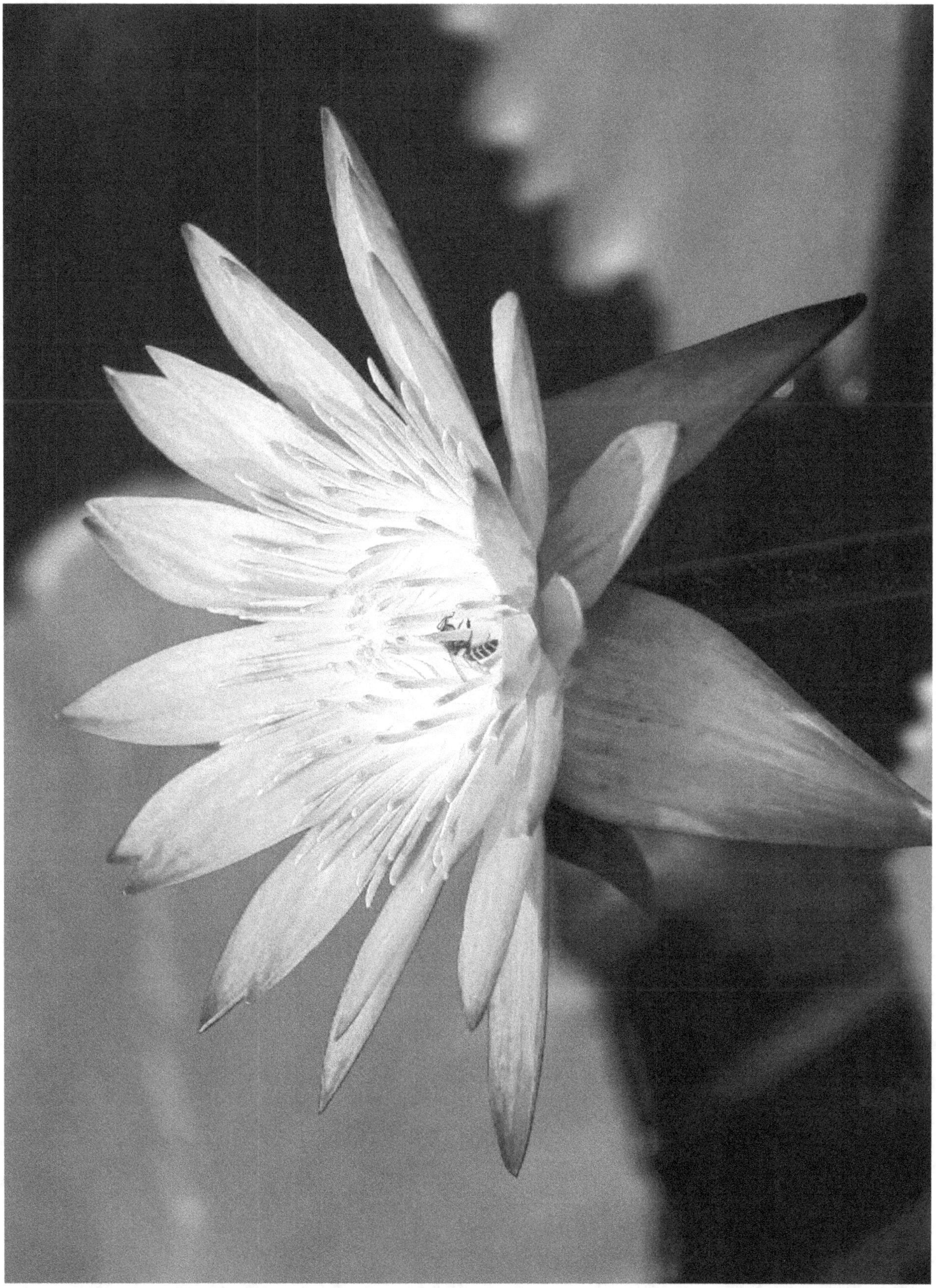

www.ingramcontent.com/pod-product-compliance
Lightning Source LLC
Chambersburg PA
CBHW081120280526
45787CB00007B/2909
* 9 7 8 1 5 3 5 0 6 8 7 1 0 *